Conversations with Teen Entrepreneurs

Conversations with Teen Entrepreneurs

✦

Success Secrets of the Younger Generation

Ben Cathers

iUniverse, Inc.
New York Lincoln Shanghai

Conversations with Teen Entrepreneurs
Success Secrets of the Younger Generation

iUniverse, Inc.

For information address:
iUniverse, Inc.
2021 Pine Lake Road, Suite 100
Lincoln, NE 68512
www.iuniverse.com

ISBN: 0-595-29410-3

Printed in the United States of America

To my parents, for their unwavering love and support for me, and my entrepreneurial endeavors.

Contents

Foreword

<u>Conversations With Teen Entrepreneurs</u> is long overdue and an extremely pertinent entry in the field of business. Currently we are seeing a greater number of young entrepreneurs and business owners than ever before. The advances in the Internet have created an unprecedented opportunity for people of all walks of life to start companies. Anyone who has access to the Internet has just about unlimited access to information. The Internet is transforming how business is done and is continuously creating new business opportunities.

The fascinating thing about the 21st Century is that transactions can take place without ever having to meet a business owner or customer. One can conduct thousands of transactions a day, through the night, over different time zones and continents without ever having to go to an office or open up shop. The Internet creates a virtual marketplace where people of all ages, educational backgrounds, languages, and income levels can be creative and generate income. Furthermore, through the Internet people can have a significant impact on the economy as well as on business, political, social and educational systems throughout the world. The Internet gives freedom to great young minds that otherwise would have had to wait until they entered the traditional workplace to share their wisdom and make their mark on society.

While a student at Cornell University I began my first entrepreneurial venture. At that time, there were few books like this one and access to information was limited. I remember working at the on-campus dining hall for a low hourly wage. By my second 4-hour shift, I realized my valuable time could be spent in a more profitable and enjoyable way.

I analyzed the Ithaca marketplace and found a gap in the market that was underserved and created a college marketing firm focusing on helping local businesses attract student customers. I investigated the marketplace and my potential competition and examined how I could best win customers. I developed a quick brand identity and a value proposition that provided customers with a greater bundle of benefits and a more cost effective offering than my competition. From there, I set a strategy to enter the market quickly and effectively. I worked hard at selling my services, but more importantly I worked hard at selling myself as a partner to Ithaca businesses.

From the beginning, I found that teen entrepreneurship afforded me unexpected opportunities. I found that my customers trusted me because I was young, sincere, passionate, and enthusiastic about my product offering. I also found my customers took a special interest in me as a young entrepreneur and took the time to explain their businesses in detail. This gave me great insight into many different business models and a close up look at the daily operations of these businesses.

Teen Entrepreneurs are in an enviable position as they transition from adolescence to adulthood. Teen entrepreneurs have access to more information at a younger age. They have the opportunity to research, interview, explore, and shadow other entrepreneurs. They have the opportunity to become a more successful entrepreneur because they have more freedom to be creative and take risks. What most people never understand is that if they do not try they will never fully know what they are capable of. Teen Entrepreneurs must realize that each opportunity is a learning experience. Successful business operators grow and evolve their skill set and business offering on an ongoing basis. All marketplaces are dynamic and the entrepreneur must learn to meet this challenge.

Entrepreneurs who take on business challenges at a young age enjoy many benefits along the way. Teen entrepreneurs who experience success at an early age generally build a confidence that perpetuates their success in the future. The more business dealings they experience now, the more savvy and prepared they will be for greater opportunities down the line.

My early entrepreneurial experiences were so powerful it empowered me to begin an entrepreneurial journey that is now entering its second decade. I still rely on today many of the contacts I established through my initial venture.

As I read this book, I was delighted to see that Ben Cathers was able to articulate his passion for entrepreneurship in a way that was educational, motivational and full of common sense and practicality. I enjoyed his discussion on some of the entrepreneurial basics including the very important discussion on Internet and Web marketing, which is an efficient and low cost entry into the business arena. The interviews between Ben and the three well-chosen entrepreneurs profiled in this book give tremendous insight into the entrepreneurial process.

I know the author to be an outstanding individual who has a remarkable thirst for knowledge and a passion for entrepreneurship. He also takes great joy in sharing and communicating his thoughts in order to help others. Although he is young, I consider him to be a very successful entrepreneur with an important message based on his experience as a true Internet Pioneer beginning at age 12. I have no doubt this book will influence others on their path to success. I look forward to watching Ben continue on his path of accomplishments.

Wishing you success,

Michael Kraner
CEO
Primary Support Solutions

Introduction

Welcome to my book, <u>Conversations with Teen Entrepreneurs</u>. I'm Ben Cathers and I am 19 years old. I have started and have successfully run two companies. One was an Internet company targeting teenagers, and the other, was a media company producing a syndicated radio show targeting the teenaged audience.

Each company brought both successes and failures. Each venture taught me lessons in business that I could only learn by going through and experiencing the highs and lows of running a company. The lessons learned have been pivotal in my success as a business student and teaching assistant at Boston University's School of Management.

So, I thought I'd write about the lessons I've learned along the way, covering my own experiences about a variety of issues, ranging from marketing issues to human resources issues. The book was to be called "Conversation with a Teen Entrepreneur." However, as I was planning the book, I continually asked colleagues of mine for advice on certain sections of the book. (Ok, at points I may have hounded them a bit). At some point during my barrage of questions, I was asked, "Who the hell is going to care what you have to say about business—you are just a teenager who ran a business or two!" Well, ok, my colleagues didn't say it exactly like that, but they had a point—who was going to listen to one teenager's advice on business? While I've accomplished a lot and I worked hard to earn the respect of everyone I've worked with, the casual reader may not feel my advice is worth anything. I thought about this (for a good solid ten minutes!) and realized that I'm not the only teenager in business (most of my colleagues are teenage entrepreneurs). I thought that, perhaps, if I included stories and advice from a group of teenaged entrepreneurs, it would add a bit more legitimacy to a book that, essentially, is a business book written by teenagers. It is directed at anyone who owns a business, is starting a business or, has a casual interest in business.

The book is sectioned into different parts. The first part of the book gives advice on different areas of business. The entrepreneurs profiled in the book provide the tips and insight. Of course, I too, provide tips and insight. Many of the tips have been tested "in the battlefields" by the entrepreneurs profiled here and myself.

The second part of the book is the "Roundtable" discussion with the entrepreneurs. In this section, the entrepreneurs engage in lengthy and exciting dialogue and answer interesting, relevant questions about themselves and their business start-ups. They reveal a lot about running their companies and overcoming their struggles in business and in their personal lives. The interviews provide a good understanding into their business practices and provide plenty of invaluable advice. The appendix holds a separate copy of each entrepreneur's personal interview.

I hope the book is an informative read. If nothing else, I hope the book provides a unique perspective into how the age barrier is changing dramatically in business.

Ben Cathers.

If you want to learn more about me or have an interest in any future books that may be published, please visit my website at http://www.bencathers.com

1

Marketing

Whether it's a billboard, an ad heard on the radio or just an advertisement in the local paper, people are exposed to marketing. Entrepreneurs understand that marketing is the key to reaching customers. Teen Entrepreneurs understand this as well, but unfortunately, all too often, their marketing budget is low. This is a common problem entrepreneurs face–wanting to reach their audience, but having a low or non-existent budget to work with. However, this has not stopped the teenaged entrepreneurs profiled here from skillfully using marketing tactics attracting attention to their businesses, and ultimately turning curious visitors into paying customers. The entrepreneurs in this book have taken advantage of online advertising & marketing and have achieved measurable results using simple, but proven tactics.

Understanding the importance of marketing

Many entrepreneurs make the fatal flaw of failing to realize the importance of marketing. Marketing is the art and science of attracting and maintaining new customers. Marketing brands your company. Devin Lazerine from Rap-up.com sums it up best, "Marketing can be the key to success when launching a new product. There should be a strong focus on it at every start up."

Planning your marketing

Before starting any type of marketing initiative or campaign, there are many things an entrepreneur must do. First, an entrepreneur must determine to whom they will be marketing to. Who is the audience? An entrepreneur must determine a broad base of customers to reach and a smaller group of "target" customers. An example of this would be choosing adults, ages 18-34 as a broad base of potential customers, and then having adult males, 18-24 as the smaller group of ideal customers. With this information, an entrepreneur can fully understand to whom he or she is marketing to, and how to avoid pitfalls. At my Internet company, we were given an opportunity to have what marketers call "A run of the network buy." In laymen's terms, this means we could purchase a large number of ads reaching anyone on the website. In other words, our ads would be seen by anyone who visited the website, whether they were a teenager (our target audience) or a 75 year old grandmother (not that we have anything against 75 year old grandmothers, but we really don't know what our website would offer them—they probably wouldn't know either). This leads to the next question:

Why would we buy these ads?

Simple. I was young and inexperienced and saw the bargain basement cost. However I committed a sin many small businesses commit—straying from one's targeted audience. There are many reasons why small businesses commit this—perhaps, because the small business is swayed by the price, or just because the small business is so desperate to advertise they will buy an advertisement on anything. When a business buys a "run of the network" ad, they are taking a crapshoot; in the best-case scenario, the people seeing the ad are the targeted audience and in the very worst-case scenario, none of the people seeing the ad are the targeted audience. Unfortunately, my situation was the latter and the $2500 my firm invested in the campaign was never recouped. For many small businesses, $2500 may very well be the entire marketing budget—so an unsuccessful campaign like this could be devastating. This was caused by straying away from our core audience and that is why it is critical to determine **who you are marketing to** and **who your advertisements are directed to.**

Ok? So now that we have that out of the way, we are going to need to plan your budget. There really is no set way to determine how much a company's overall spending marketing budget should be. For some businesses, the only way to acquire new customers and to retain customers is through marketing. Businesses such as retail stores and food stores continuously need to advertise and therefore spend a large portion of their budget on advertising. Other firms, such as service firms with clients who tend to have large budgets, may not necessarily need to dedicate a large portion of their budget on marketing. And of course, there will always be firms like HotJobs.com, which reportedly spent half of their budget buying a super bowl advertisement that paid off big-time (and eventually spawned a bunch of wannabe companies who spent large portions of their overall budgets on super bowl advertisements and subsequently went out of business).

How do I determine what portion of my budget should be dedicated towards advertising?

There are several rules of thumb to go by. My personal favorite is to determine how much of a necessity the product is and how loyal your customers are. If a business is a food store selling the same products as four or five other stores in the area, they may not necessarily have loyal customers. Therefore, they will need to continuously spend on marketing in order to retain your customers. In other businesses, the customers are incredibly loyal and no advertisement will make them leave their current place of business. It is best to examine the particular situation and evaluate the above criteria. If a business falls into the middle, then they will need to talk with customers, look at what other competitors are doing, and make a decision based on those results. **Remember, one solution that is good for one business may not be good for another.**

On the other hand, if someone is a new business, they are going to need to dedicate a significant portion of their budget on marketing **just to get their name out.** An entrepreneur starting a new business needs to focus his/her marketing efforts on getting its name out to potential customers. He then must determine his customers' behaviors after viewing the advertisement. If the business is advertising in offline advertising (meaning any sort of advertising not involved on the Internet) it is hard to track what the customer is doing. The best way will be by actually speaking to the customer and getting his feedback on the ad. If the business is advertising online, it is easier to track the results; it is how many of the entrepreneurs in this book succeeded. The entrepreneurs were able to spend their money on advertising/marketing, determine what the customer was doing when they viewed the ad and subsequently was able to alter their marketing efforts based on that information.

Now that we have all of the necessary prerequisites for starting up a marketing campaign, we will now focus on online advertising. Some comments on "traditional" forms of advertising will be noted in the end, but for the entrepreneurs profiled in this book, online advertising proved to be the most cost effective and successful way of advertising—but only because they chose the right solution(s) for their businesses. A word of caution, it is very easy to spend thousands of dollars on online marketing and not generate any tangible leads.

Search Engine Marketing

One of the preferred methods of finding information on the Internet is through search engines. By being smart and understanding how search engines work, entrepreneurs can tap into a large amount of free traffic. The search engine game is a very complicated one and it often takes a good amount of research and reading to be able to fully master the ability to gain a high ranking. An entire guide to search engine positioning can be hundreds of pages. However, here are some tips that all entrepreneurs should know:

-Make full use of the <meta> description and keywords (ask a web designer if you are unfamiliar with this). Make sure your description of your site is around 20 words and the keywords of your site are around 20-30.

-Make sure the keywords are targeted to the business. Do not put in general keywords such as "happy, hello, yeah" if they are irrelevant to the business. It will damage the firm's ability to gain a better ranking.

-Put keywords/description in your ALT tags on the images (once again, speak with a web designer if unfamiliar with this).

-Make sure the site has substantive and **relative** content to the keywords and descriptions. Search engines frown upon the site when the site's keywords conflict with the rest of the site's content.

Make sure to take advantage of the plethora of information on the Internet regarding search engine optimization and positioning. Some of the best sites for information include:

-SearchEngineWatch.com. An amazing resource for anyone serious about learning about search engine positioning. Many of the articles are free, but the site also has a premium section.

-SearchEngineForums.com. A great search engine forum that I am a member of. Excellent resource where you can ask the very intelligent moderators and members questions about search engine positioning and get strong answers. Excellent resource for people new to the game who have a lot of questions.

Now, if all of the search engine positioning sounds like a lot of work, there is a new trend called "pay-per-click search engines" that eliminate all the grunt work of establishing a high search engine placement. With these search engines, firms do what the name suggests–pay for the search engine rank. While some keywords go for ridiculous prices (going as high as $3.00 a click) if a firm is smart and knows what they are doing, then firms can still find some true bargains on these search engines.

Pay Per Click Search Engines

This craze can be attributed to GoTo.com (now called Overture, which has been acquired by Yahoo!). GoTo.com was the pioneer in pay-per-click search engines. Hundreds of imitators were spawned as a result of GoTo.com's outstanding success. Some of the better-known pay-per-click search engines include Find-What.com; Kanoodle.com; Sprinks.com; ePilot.com; 7search.com and search123.com. There are many more out there; do a search on Google.com or The Open Directory (dmoz.org) to find listings of other pay per click search engines out there. The value proposal of pay-per-click search engines is that firms are able to place a bid to gain a high search engine position. Let's say a site wants to be the first site that comes up on the keyword "Baseball." A firm would use one of the search engine listing tools provided by the pay-per-click search engines and check out how much the bid is. For argument's sake, let's say the bid is 15 cents. What this means is that every time a web surfer searches for the term "baseball" on that particular search engine and clicks on the link, the person who owns the website using that term pays 15 cents to the pay-per-click search engine. Now, if a site wants to be the #1 site that comes up, they would put a bid of 16 cents and if your site is approved (it isn't necessarily hard to be approved, but the search engines have an approval process to prevent, for example, websites about sharks being the #1 site to come up when someone searches for baseball). You are now the #1 site listed on the term "baseball." Pretty neat huh?

Ok, so now firms have a good idea of pay-per-click search engines. Before firms sign up, they must establish a battle plan before signing up with a couple of search engines. Most pay-per-click search engines require a minimum account deposit, varying from 1 dollar to 50 dollars. Firms should make sure to have enough money budgeted so they can test the waters with at least two or three pay-per-click search engines. I have discovered that just because one pay-per-click search engine is the leader, it may not be the best. If firms look hard enough, they will find pay-per-click search engines with comparable amounts of traffic for their keyword at a fraction of the cost of other pay-per-click search engines. **Firms should make sure to research all the search engines and get a good idea of what the rates are.** Now, after firms have done a little bit of research, it will be necessary to determine the keywords.

Let's imagine that the website is an online baseball memorabilia store. The owner of the site will obviously want a high ranking under the keyword "baseball." But be forewarned, generic and popular words, such as baseball, often have bids. It is imperative to determine at what price it is profitable to pay for one visitor to your website. While the owner may have his/her eyes set on being the first site that comes up whenever someone searches for the term "baseball" it may not be economical to put down a bid of 85 cents for the keyword. Instead, examine what price the site in the #2 spot is paying as well as the price of the #3 spot and so forth. It is not always necessary to gain the #1 spot. Sometimes positioning as the 4th or 5th site will perform just as well as a site in the #1 spot. Even a position as low as the 18th spot may perform well if the keyword is popularly searched (the person performing the search may have already seen the first couple of sites and is looking for a new website to visit). Also, another method to getting the best bang for your buck is to examine alternative keywords. Less popular, but more targeted keywords such as "baseball memorabilia" or "baseball autographs" may have more attractive bid prices and may also bring **higher quality visitors to your site** (a person searching under the word "baseball" may not be necessarily looking for baseball memorabilia, as opposed to someone searching under the term "baseball autographs"). In this situation, it is crucial for the site owner to become creative and "think out of the box" in order to determine the best keywords for his site.

Don't let this advice go to waste. Bryan Hammond of ExploreAnywhere Software LLC relies on pay-per-click search engines to bring in the bulk of his website traffic. A large portion of his customers came after searching on a search engine and a pay-per-click search engine.

There are many other ways to market online, but many of them can be costly and may not be the most attractive to budding entrepreneurs. However, it is advisable for firms to be looking around at other websites in the market and look at the advertising rates. Firms should make deals with friendly competitors to swap website links. They should try to get their site on as many other sites as possible. **Firms never know when a curious web surfer may stumble on their site and becoming a paying customer.** Firms must always be prepared for this type of situation, which leads me nicely into the next area of marketing.

What do you do when someone visits the website?

This is a very important area to analyze. Getting traffic to a firm's website is winning half the battle–the other half is understanding what happens when someone visits the website. You may receive one million visits a day, but if the website is not actively making the business money, then the visits mean nothing. That became true for many of the teen entrepreneurs profiled in this book. The web presence has helped to make or break their businesses. Just listen to Devin Lazerine of Rap-up, "The internet has opened up so many doors for me. If not for the net, I would probably not have a magazine. The Internet gave me the opportunity to have a website and reach a large amount of people."

A little later on we will focus on the many issues regarding website development and how to make the Internet presence work.

Other forms of advertising

The teenagers in this book have had limited experience in using other forms of advertising/marketing to help build their business. Most have found online advertising and marketing to be the essentials in building a business. Many of the ideas and suggestions in this chapter can be applied to the other forms of available advertising.

In my radio show, I had many different sponsors. I dealt with some who sponsored for the sole purpose of advertising on the radio. It added prestige to their business, so they say. But three months later, when the sponsors complained about a lack of results, they only had themselves to blame. Many inexperienced entrepreneurs believe that if they advertise on any form of media, they will generate results. This ignores the basic idea of knowing **whom the target market is** and **how to reach that market.** Buying 30 radio ads blindly may expose a business to many new customers, but if the product is a wheelchair aimed at senior citizens and it is being advertised on a children's program, it will most likely generate poor, if any results. (Though perhaps a few grandparents watching their grandchildren may buy in). An entrepreneur must treat their advertising purchase as an investment. Perform due diligence. Research the market. Negotiate better prices. Go into the purchase hoping for the best while expecting the worse. A new candy may be very appealing to teenagers, and advertising on a teenaged related program may seem like a dream buy, but understand it's not a definite. The person purchasing the advertisement has to understand this. There may be a definite match, but ultimately, it is up to the consumer to decide how they will spend their hard earned money. The candy market may be over saturated. There may be little demand from the teenaged segment for a new candy product. If a business is selling candy to an audience that is already satisfied with their current candy choices, the business faces a daunting task in reaching them. Research, research, and research some more!

Devin Lazerine of Rap-Up leaves us with his own experiences on advertising. "We have used television, Internet, and print marketing. Television exposed the product to the largest amount of people and we received the biggest response from that. The Internet is useful because people can always find out about you and the website is there as a tool. Print has proven to be helpful, but not as much as TV."

Chatting with Bryan Hammond on Internet Marketing

Bryan Hammond, the CEO of Explore Anywhere Software, has been using Internet marketing to help develop new leads for his software business. Bryan contributes must of his success to Internet marketing. Bryan has gladly offered to give some advice and insight into how he used the Internet to create new customers.

Q. How do you use online marketing to build your business?

Bryan Hammond: I use online marketing to bring exposure to the company and the software developed.

Q. What types of online advertising do you use?

Bryan Hammond: I have used pay per clicks, advertising on download sites, links on sites, etc.

Q. What is the most cost effective kind of online advertising?

Bryan Hammond: The most effective form of advertising would be search engines, because it is directly targeted to the market you are in (because your advertising revolves around keywords).

Q. Can you track your ROI (Return on Investment) from your campaigns?

Bryan Hammond: That is too difficult because of my affiliates.

Q. What are affiliates? How are you using them to boost your business?

Bryan Hammond: Affiliates sell the software for a commission. They boost the business for obvious reasons. The more people selling your product and marketing it, the more sales come in more of a name is built up for your company cause people see the software everywhere.

Q. Have you used any other forms of advertising besides online advertising?

Bryan Hammond: Nope, I haven't done anything other than online advertising.

Q, Why don't you use any other forms of advertising?

Bryan Hammond: In my market, it's most cost effective to use online advertising because of the nature of the product. I get more results from online ads.

Q. Can you give any tips to anyone interested in starting an online advertising campaign? What is a good way to start?

Bryan Hammond: Search engines. Without a doubt, start buying keywords on search engines. You can target a specific audience and pay only for your results. Make sure to research your keywords and then look at other search engines and see who can give you the best deal. Check factors such as price for pay-per-click, paid placements, etc. It costs money upfront, but you will see results from the money.

Q. What's the best marketing tip you can tell u?

Bryan Hammond: You got to spend money to make money. Do legitimate advertising, and don't fall for "too good to be true" schemes (like 10 millions hits to your website in a day, etc). These schemes give your business a bad reputation, and give rarely any results. The best advertising is done by reaching your audience (in every aspect) and finding related websites, magazines, etc that offer advertising plans.

Chatting with Aaron Greenspan of Think Computer Corporation in regard to marketing

Q. What is the most cost effective method of marketing you have used?

Aaron Greenspan: Word-of-mouth and the press are the two most cost-effective methods of marketing in existence.

Q. Can you list all the forms of marketing you have used and tell of their effectiveness?

Aaron Greenspan: Word-of-mouth—Very high
Trade shows and conferences—Poor
Networking groups—Poor
Press articles—Very high
Print advertising—Poor
Web advertising—Very Poor
E-mail—Average

Q. What's the best marketing tip you can tell?

Aaron Greenspan: Don't pay for anything if you don't have to.

2

The Internet

Every single entrepreneur profiled in this book has had some experience with the Internet. The entrepreneurs use the Internet to help run their business; use it as an extension of their business; or base their entire enterprise on the Internet. It is critical for anyone with as much as a passing interest in business to understand the importance of the Internet. The previous chapter dealt with online marketing strategies, this chapter will discuss how to use the Internet to a business owner's advantage, and how to make the web presence of the business a successful one.

It is important to make use of the many free and low cost solutions out there on the Internet. While Instant Messaging (IM) has been mostly used among people who want to stay in touch, if used correctly it is one of the most important tools for businesses. When allowing employees to use an IM tool, firms need to set ground rules. Make sure the tool is being used for business and not for personal chit chat that could lose productivity at the office (this is a major problem with many corporations). Firms should establish IM accounts for everyone in the office. Firms should see if business partners also have IM names. This will allow people to stay in touch with their clients and have instant communication. Offices in different cities, states or even countries can communicate with each other in a matter of seconds. Barriers to communication are broken down with just a few simple programs. The same goes for email, but firms should make sure email is treated as a professional medium. While it is easy to have typos and to use slang in an email, spending an additional five or ten seconds and proofreading the email is an easy way for firms to avoid those mistakes. Firms should format emails correctly. Nothing looks more unprofessional than a business proposal that is full of typos, or has incorrect grammar usage (it is not there house, it is their house).

Smart entrepreneurs understand this. The teenagers profiled in this book also took advantage of this. Whether it was something simple such as sending an instant message to an employee while they were home, or using email as a solicitation tool for new business, the Internet helped to streamline business processes for the entrepreneurs. Sending out five emails to potential partners and getting a response that day is far more effective (both coastwise and time wise) than sending out a "snail mail" (a letter sent via the postal service). However, there is a need for snail mail. Sending a letter via the postal service shows the business took time in preparation and went the "extra mile" to impress the recipient. Nothing makes a current partner smile more than a creative letter sent via the postal service. A 37-cent stamp and an envelope can go a long way–a smart entrepreneur understands the balance between email and snail mail and will be able to determine when which one is appropriate.

It is also important to see how the Internet can solve any dilemma. It is important to identify the problem and explore how the problem can be solved. After getting a good idea of some sort of panacea to the business ailment, it is crucial to explore possible solutions on the Internet. Often, these solutions can be implemented at low costs (or lower costs than the current pricing situation) and are relatively easy to grasp. The entrepreneurs profiled in this book did just that. Bryan Hammond, CEO of ExploreAnywhere Software LLC has been using Internet applications to help reduce the time and effort, as well as costs that come with customer service. "The internet gives me the ability to assist customers via the web in a timely manner, without having to spend money on a phone support staff."

While the Internet is not a "cure-all" to all business problems, it is important to seek out solutions on the web. It can alleviate a few headaches, and also cut costs dramatically. If someone can't find a solution to your problem in the form of an Internet based solution, well, then there have a potential new business idea right there!

The web presence

When a business or entrepreneur first establishes a web presence, they are establishing an important part of their business. One of the key items is to get a domain name (this is essentially your businessname.com/.net/.org). Previously, it was costly to get a domain name, but now that there are many domain name registering companies (previously there was only one). Registration can cost as little as $6.99 (or even less). Firms such as godaddy.com or web.com offer domain names at great prices. After a business or entrepreneur establishes a domain name, they are ready to establish their web presence. There are many keys and rules for entrepreneurs and businesses to follow to ensure they have the most efficient web presence as possible.

One of the most important parts of a web presence is understanding the customers and understanding customers' needs. Any business or entrepreneur needs to see what rival businesses are doing on the Internet and see what is working and what is not working. It is important to know the types of customers so the entrepreneur knows what type of website to have. In some businesses, a site with "all the bells and whistles" with fancy graphics and fancy animations may be the best. Other times, a simple website with relatively few graphics and content may be important. It really depends on the customers' wants and needs. For example, amazon.com needs a relatively simple design (few graphics and no animations) and a rather cluttered design to show off their massive offerings. Amazon.com also needs extra pages on authors, different genres, recommendations, etc. On the other hand, a graphic design firm will require less text/content and require fancy animations and impressive graphics so the firm can show off their skills. Every web presence is relative to the needs of the business and its customers.

It is now time to get to the heart of the matter–what to do when someone comes to visit an entrepreneur's website and to understand how to turn them into a potentially paying client. The first and most important thing is to treat the visitor to your business website as a potential customer. It is the same as when someone walks into a store and takes a look around. The visitor is a potential customer and unless the visitor was forced to the site beyond their will or accidentally typed in the wrong address (and stumbled upon the entrepreneur's site) the visitor came because they are interested in the products/services offered by the business. Therefore, it is crucial to make the web visitors experience at the site an enjoyable one.

One of the key points is to not undermine the visitor's intelligence. Inundating the user with annoying pop-up ads (and forcing the visitor to play a game which involves opening and closing the pop-up ads) is a perfect way to anger the visitor. Content is one of the most important items a web site can have. By helping to educate the user about a business' services or providing more information about the industry, the business is adding to the knowledge of the visitor. By adding an extra value to the website, the business already has a competitive advantage over competitors. If the business is a graphic design firm, having a few extra pages about the graphic design process will help to educate the visitor and give the visitor a better insight into the services offered by the business. Additionally, a site such as Amazon.com offers visitors' reviews of its books and extra features such as sample chapters and visitor reviews, giving the visitor a better idea of the book and whether or not it is a potential addition to the visitor's library. Once again, the type of content a website may offer is relative to the industry/business the website is focusing on. But one thing remains clear, is vital to offer additional information to make the website stand out from the sea of competitor sites. Devin from Rap Up agrees that content is king, "A major pitfall with most websites is that people don't update their sites on a regular basis and that can be a problem. Visitors want content that is up-to-date and maintained regularly."

Stickiness refers to how long a visitor stays at a website. This is an important measure to a website's effectiveness. Often stickiness can be measured by viewing a website's statistics. Many website statistics programs will tell how long a visitor stays at the site, how many pages the average visitor visits and what pages the visitor left at (the exit pages). It is important for any business maintaining a web presence to read over these statistics at least once a week and identify any problems. Businesses need to ask themselves "Why is the person leaving at this page?" or "How can we better accommodate the visitor?" Improving simple things like this may very well lead to additional customers. By discovering what is making the visitor unhappy, a business is able to identify a problem and fix it. This kind of research is very expensive, but with a website and the right website statistics program (most companies who are in the business of hosting websites will offer some sort of statistics program–it is best to ask the ISP or web-host) this type of research is available for free or at a very low cost.

One of the prevailing themes of this chapter is how a website can be used to access information about customers and better understand the customers. Therefore, it is important for businesses to take advantage of many of the research tools available on the Internet. There are many free and low cost audience measurement tools available. With as little as ten minutes of effort, websites can offer polls to their visitors. These polls can offer questions about products, buying habits, etc, etc. It is best to offer some sort of incentive (such as anyone who takes the poll is automatically entered into a contest to win a 50 dollar gift certificate). This encourages more responses to the poll. From there, businesses and entrepreneurs can learn directly **from their customers** about what they want to see improved, and what the visitors would like to see from their business. Entrepreneurs/businesses that are not doing this are not maximizing their web presence. Period.

Creating the web presence

This chapter has detailed what to do with a business' web presence and how to fully maximize a web presence. However, we have not yet explored in any great detail, how to create a web presence. So we will now conclude the chapter with information on how to establish a web presence. For many, creating web sites is a hobby–some are good, some are bad, and some are amazing. For others, creating websites is a full time occupation. For me, it started out as a hobby that has developed into much more.

Understanding the languages

All websites are made with a programming language called "HTML." HTML stands for Hypertext Markup Language. HTML is considered by many programmers to be the easiest programming language to learn–some don't even call it a programming language because of its simplicity. HTML is one of the languages and takes about two hours to learn, but takes a lot of time to master. To learn more about HTML and how to program in it, my personal favorite site is http:// www.htmlgoodies.com. Picking up any book on HTML is also a smart idea.

The other commonly used programming languages include Perl, Java, JavaScript, Dynamic HTML (DHTML), PHP, Cold Fusion and a score of others. For all intensive purposes, it is only necessary to know what these languages do. Perl is one programming language used to make a website more interactive. Many message boards, guest books, email systems, etc etc are made with Perl. These interactive systems are also made in PHP and Cold Fusion. Java is a programming language designed by Sun Microsystems that can be used to create advanced applications and can also be used to create flashy web animations. Speaking of web animations, Flash and Shockwave, created by Macromedia; create fully interactive and graphically intense online movies. JavaScript and DHTML are used to create interactive menus on the website and interactive parts of the site that are less complex than the interactive programs created in PERL/Cold Fusion and PHP.

Now that we have gotten the different types of languages out of the way, it is time to create the web presence. For some businesses that are heavily reliant on their website, it is important to have an in-house web team. This means there should be a staff of anywhere from one to one hundred people whose sole purpose is to maintain the website. If a website requires daily updates and constant additions to the site, it may be necessary to have an in-house web team. But an in-house web team doesn't have to be expensive–often interns can handle these types of tasks and would be more than happy to do something other than stapling and answering calls.

If a business decides to outsource the website, the business would contract the website out to a professional design firm. These firms can cost as low as 100 dollars and go upwards of 100,000 or even more. It all depends on who the firm is and what type of requirements the business has for their website. When picking a web design firm, a business often "gets what they paid for". That means a business with a 100 dollar website may not be as impressive as a business with a 100,000 dollar website. But this doesn't necessarily always hold true. There are many "starving designers" who will create an impressive looking website at low prices. There are also many web design firms out there who design websites at high prices and aren't worth anything. It is very important for a business, when selecting a web design firm, to ask and check out references. Examine the portfolio of websites. Ask if the firm is familiar with the different programming languages out there. Will the firm charge by the hour or per site? Is the firm familiar with search engine positioning? Will the firm re-design the site if the owner doesn't like it? Will the firm provide the necessary tools needed for the owner to update the website? Is there a fee associated with updating the site? The last two questions are important because if the web designer provides the tools necessary to update the website, it may be possibly to outsource the website and then after it is completed, be able to have the rest of the website provided in-house. With this, a firm can obtain an affordable web presence and then maintain the rest of the site in-house, thereby lowering costs. This is exactly what Devin from Rap-Up did with the Rap-up.com website "The website was developed both in-house and with freelancers." This helped Devin manage the website as an extension of the magazine, thereby adding more value to the entire business.

Choosing a web host

A web-host is where a business' website is located. After a website is created and a domain name is secured, a business needs a place on a server to maintain its website. Businesses that are in need of large, high trafficked websites will often buy their own server and have their own technicians take care of it. But for most businesses this is not a necessity. Often, businesses will buy space from a server at a fixed rate. Depending on the needs of the business, web space with a web-host can go anywhere from $1.99 a month to $99.99 a month. Once again, it is all relative to the business' needs. The best places to look for a web-host are ISPCheck.com and Hostsearch.com. When searching for a web-host, it is important to understand these key terms:

Bandwidth–This is how much website transfer a website can have. For example, let's say a business orders a web-hosting package that allows 1 gigabyte of transfer a month. Lets also say the business has a website which is 1 megabyte (very large for a website) in size. Every time there is a visit to the website, 1 megabyte of transfer occurs. This means, the website is allowed to have 1,000 visitors. After the monthly quota of bandwidth occurs, two things usually occur. Either the web-host will turn off the site for the rest of the month (to prevent any more traffic from happening) or will began to charge the website extra fees for the traffic. These extra fees vary by web-host. It is very important to get an estimate of a site's traffic, the size of the files that will be on the web-host and to know how much bandwidth there is included with a web hosting plan. It is also important to know the web-host policies if a website exceeds its monthly bandwidth allowance. Also, be very cautious with web-hosts offering "unlimited bandwidth". Often, when reading the fine print of a contract, it will state that if the website receives an incredibly large amount of traffic, the unlimited bandwidth will be removed and the website will be charged accordingly.

POP3 Email–This is the email account associated with the domain name. When a business gets a domain name, it will want an email address associated with a domain name. Running a business with a free yahoo or hotmail account is very unprofessional. Look to see how many pop3 accounts are included with an account and see how many are needed for the organization (if there are 15 people in the business who need a pop3 account and the web hosting plan only offers 10, then there is a problem)

UNIX or NT Server–This is the more technical part of the site. Some web designers prefer working with a UNIX server and some prefer working with a Windows NT server. Make sure to check with the in-house web team or the web designer to see what their preference is. Certain Perl scripts will work with UNIX servers but may not work with Windows NT servers.

Microsoft Frontpage Extensions–If the web designer or someone in the organization creates and updates the website with Microsoft Frontpage, this is essential. If not, move along.

Disk Storage–This is how many megabytes of files a business may have on the web-host. Businesses need to check and see how much space their website takes up and if the organization will be using the web space to upload important files or articles.

Database Support–For more technical websites, a Microsoft SQL server or equivalent will be required to maintain certain applications. Businesses should check with their designers or the programs they are using to see if this is a necessity.

There are many other options a web-host will include. Many are worthless and some are vital to a business. If a business is unsure of some of the options included with their website, or doesn't see the features it needs, then contact the web-host. The majority of web-hosts will be glad to answer any questions as the web-host market is over saturated and it is definitely a buyer's market in terms of web-host plans.

These are just some of the important items to check out when first establishing a web presence. It is often recommended to read up more about the subject or to talk with a qualified consultant to fully establish a profitable, moneymaking web presence.

Discussion on the Internet with Bryan Hammond (ExploreAnywhere Software) and Aaron Greenspan (Think Computer Corporation)

Q. How has the Internet changed your business?

Aaron Greenspan: Think Computer probably would never have happened without the Internet. Much of the information I found about starting a business was only available to me through the World Wide Web. Many of my customers have found me through the Internet, and some would not even be customers if the Internet did not exist since they purchase internet-related goods and services. At the present time, all of the software products that we sell to customers are web-based.

Bryan Hammond: It has allowed me capture the eyes of billions of people. The Internet is a great thing—without it, I doubt the business would be as successful as it is.

Q. How are you using the Internet to add value to your business?

Aaron Greenspan: Customers can purchase Think Computer products and services over our secure web site using a credit card at http://www.thinkcomputer.com.

Bryan Hammond: I use the Internet to market products, find ideas, advertise, etc.

Q. How did you develop your web presence? In house or outsourced?

Aaron Greenspan: I taught myself HTML in seventh grade, and Think Computer has had about eight versions of its corporate web site since then. We host our own web site, as well as many others.

Bryan Hammond: The website was designed by my graphic designer, but I plugged in all of the content, etc. I like to do things on my own because I am very picky. Plus, I know where to strategically place things to help entice sales and whatnot.

Q. What's a pitfall most people face with their website?

Aaron Greenspan: Most small businesses cannot afford an in-house Information Technology staff, and therefore have to rely on a site designer to make updates for them. Designers know this, and often charge outrageous rates to update sites as a result. We've developed Whiteboard, a program geared toward small businesses, to allow people to update their own web sites without any outside help. With a retail price of $99.00, it's much more affordable than practically any other solution on the market.

Bryan Hammond: Image is everything. If your site is garbage, you won't get sales. You need to pay attention to detail. If you aren't good at designing websites, hire someone that is. If your web-presence isn't good enough, people won't trust you, and thus, people will not buy from you.

Q. How do you see the Internet affecting your business?

Bryan Hammond: As the Internet grows, so does the concern of cheating spouses, employees getting off task, children talking to pedophiles, etc. All of these things are what makes my software so popular. Controversy sells. And it just so happens that my software relates directly to what everyone uses on a daily basis (the internet, chatting, etc) so it is unlikely that the Internet will cause the business to go under.

3

Negotiations

One of the most daunting tasks any entrepreneur must do is to enter negotiations. Whether the negotiations are to secure a new client, raise capital for a firm or even to close any current business deals, negotiations are often stressful and difficult. For the teenaged entrepreneurs featured in this book, negotiations were even more difficult. Faced with all the difficulties that are generally associated with negotiations, the teenaged entrepreneurs also were dealt with an additional handicap–proving they were worthy enough to be in the meeting.

Dealing with potential clients

This is one of the most common forms of negotiations the entrepreneurs in this book faced. While many of the entrepreneurs profiled had dealt with negotiations on a smaller scale basis previously (i.e., working at a McDonalds and negotiating a meal with a customer) none of them had experience dealing with corporate customers and for the amounts they were negotiating for. It was virgin territory and is an area most entrepreneurs face.

When entering new client negotiations, one of the most important and obvious tips is to fully understand and know the client. Research the company. Research the industry. Research the competitors. It is vital to know the industry and to understand the needs of the industry. Not only will the potential client be impressed by the knowledge, but also the firm will be able to offer solutions relative and vital to the potential client. The entrepreneur should prepare answers to potential questions that the potential client might ask. If you can, role-play with a friend or colleague. You don't want to be stumbling and grasping for answers out of the thin air, be prepared! Another potential disaster is when an entrepreneur shows a lack of confidence. This will be a prevailing theme as confidence is key. Devin from Rap-Up agrees, "You have to be confident when negotiating. If you don't seem confident when discussing your business, then it won't look like you have confidence in your product." Taking the view of the person in charge of making the purchase, would they rather purchase from someone who is nervous and stumbling over questions, without a clue about the industry or from someone who comes in, looking professional, speaking professional and very confident, with a strong knowledge of the industry? Simple theories like this, however, seem to evade many entrepreneurs. Often the confidence issue is something that can be accomplished with practice and getting a strong "feel of the deal." Knowledge about the industry is something that can be done with research.

Dealing with investors

One of the most stressful events any entrepreneur must endure is dealing with finance people. This is why many entrepreneurs try to self-fund or "bootstrap" (run the organization as lean as possible). However, many entrepreneurs will seek some sort of financial assistance. Whether it is a loan to get operations back to normal after unexpected problems or venture capital to help get a business "to the next level," many entrepreneurs will be faced with the daunting task of dealing with investors.

When dealing with investors, confidence is going to be key. Many investors will attempt to break down entrepreneurs and gauge their reactions. Investors will ask hundreds of questions, with each getting more difficult while expecting qualified responses for each question. Even if an entrepreneur is unsure of the answer, it is important to be able to answer the question to his best ability and with the best delivery. I was involved in an investor meeting where for three hours I was grilled with question after question. I had to repeat many answers and was often required to re-read parts of the business plan (and the research) to validate my answers. The questions got more specific and it almost seemed like a game to the investors. Luckily, at the end, things calmed down and the meeting ended with a handshake and promise to talk further. I can easily attribute that to my ability to answer questions under pressure–even though my confidence was shot afterwards, I had it while in the meeting–and that is when it counted. Subsequently, when I talked with the investors, they told me they were impressed with my answers, even though they felt that some my answers were outright wrong (and they had the evidence to pack up that claim). They said I was cool, calm and collected–and that is exactly what they are looking for.

It is critical to understand non-verbal communication. All too often I was in meetings where I was thinking one way, but if I understood the non-verbal actions of the participants, I would have been thinking the other way (and the right way). Often, understanding non-verbal communication can help an entrepreneur shift the conversation. If the entrepreneur is talking about something and is able to understand, through non-verbal communication, that the person(s) he is pitching to are uninterested in the conversation, then the entrepreneur is at an advantage and understands that he should shift the conversation around.

Figuring out equipment problems and technology issues is vital. When an investor requests a business plan, the entrepreneur needs to make sure the format he sends it in is compatible with the investors computer. Entrepreneurs should take advantage of Adobe PDF, which is basically the cure-all to any sort of incompatibility issues when dealing with any type of written document. Also, it is unprofessional for an entrepreneur to take out time to fiddle around with projection screens and computers. If it is possible for an entrepreneur to bring a projection screen which he knows is compatible with the potential investor's technology, then he should do so to avoid any incompatibility problem.

Entrepreneurs should make sure to follow-up after the initial meeting. Entrepreneurs need to understand that many investors deal with hundreds of meetings and hundreds of business plans–it is very possible for an investor to overlook and forget about a meeting. Entrepreneurs need to follow up, ask if there is anything they can do to serve them, and should follow up on any requests of information from the meeting. Nothing looks better than an entrepreneur who took time to research the requested items, delivered it in a professional format and offered to set aside time to discuss anything else. If an entrepreneur makes it easier for investors to deal with them, then many investors will reciprocate and make it easier to deal with them. This is professional courtesy at its best.

Dealing with potential employees

Every single company wants to hire only the best and brightest. After all, if the company invests in every employee, then the company wants to achieve the highest return possible. Large companies are able to attract the best and brightest because they can afford to pay salaries that are very appealing to the employees and are able to offer a multitude of luxuries that will be of great benefit to the potential hire. Many entrepreneurs want to hire only the best and brightest, but start-ups and small businesses cannot afford to offer the benefits that the best and brightest can command. It is a nasty double-edged sword.

When an entrepreneur enters into negotiations with potential employees, they need to underscore the importance and the potential of the business. When I was running my radio show, we were looking to hire some of the best advertising sales people around, but we could barely afford to offer $1/10^{th}$ any of these talented employees could receive from top firms. When I talked to them, I had to make it clear the type of environment they would be working in (that was one of our strongest advantages–the potential employee had a lot more freedom than at a large firm) and clearly state that the employee was on the ground level of something huge. I had a lot of excitement (probably too much) and I had to share that excitement to the potential employee. I wanted the employee to be able to go down the street and say, "I'm working at Ben's Radio Show—This is so exciting!" I also had to explain that their success dictated the money they could make– something that is true at a lot of start-ups, but not necessarily true at a lot of large firms. We grew because of the hard work and loyalty of our employees. Their diligence reaped the benefits; we were able to offer and afford better benefits and a higher salary for our employees. They were in charge of their own destiny–what they did not only made a difference to the company, but made a difference to themselves.

4

Success

One of the best quotes I've ever heard was by Michael Kraner, CEO of Primary Support Solutions (a firm I worked at in the summer of 2003 and, now am contracted with as a marketing consultant), "Every overnight success is at least 10 years in the making." This is very true. While it seems like many of the profiled teens achieved success at an early age, it is only through hard work and plenty of sweat and tears that success was achieved. Granted, it didn't take the entrepreneurs profiled in this book ten years, but they didn't start a business and wake up the next day rich. For me, it took almost three years before I was able to earn my first check from my business. It took four years before I found a partner for my first venture. Luckily, I was living with my parents and didn't have to worry about expenses, such as rent, food, etc. But many budding entrepreneurs are not as fortunate as me; I was able to develop my entrepreneurial endeavors and not have to worry about daily life expenses. Therefore, the sacrifices early entrepreneurs make may often have detrimental effects on their lifestyle, psychological well-being, relationships, etc. Entrepreneurs who leave the finance/corporate world to start their own business are often giving up a 6 or even 7 figure job and making instead, perhaps, $30,000 a year, or if they are lucky, $50,000 a year (depending on how well capitalized the venture is) or maybe, if not so lucky, nothing. Such a drastic change in lifestyle affects most anyone. That's why entrepreneurial-ship is not for everyone.

Planning for success

Entrepreneurs need to set goals and milestones for their businesses. These milestones need to be realistic with set and flexible projected dates of completion. Unrealistic goals (which are set, unfortunately, all too often) lead to unrealistic expectations and delusions of grandeur. Unrealistic goals often lead to despair when the business is unable to meet these goals. Businesses should not depend on unrealistic goals to help move along a business' objective. If a startup is planning on selling 100 million dollars worth of goods within its first year and doesn't achieve that goal, it will not break even and eventually go out of business; something, obviously then was seriously flawed with the business model.

It is crucial for businesses to establish realistic goals and deadlines. If a business doesn't reach a self imposed goal, the business must examine its current situation–while still having cash left in the bank to make the changes necessary to alleviate the problem(s). This will force a business to ask itself "Why didn't we achieve this goal?" and "What are the problems surrounding this?" By being forced to ask these questions, it can then locate the root of the problem and take preventative measures so that a small problem does not evolve into a huge disaster.

Many of the teen entrepreneurs started their businesses out of their bedrooms solely because they were looking for "something to do." All too often, something that started as a hobby turns into something much more. When people go out and start something solely for the purpose of making money, people will often fall on their face (unless the idea is revolutionary). Entrepreneurs must create personal and professional objectives for running the business (other than profit-making). Some questions a new entrepreneur may want to explore are: Do you get satisfaction from running the business? Do you feel a sense of purpose when managing other people? Is there a genuine thrill in making a business decision—or attending a meeting? Personally, I've never set out to make money in my ventures; I started the businesses because I loved what I was doing (honestly). I enjoyed what I was doing and got a thrill off of doing a business deal–designing a website, being part of a team. The monetary gain came later and was also very enjoyable–but if my sole purpose were for monetary gain, I would have had a very unhappy first couple of years. All too often I have seen entrepreneurs and colleagues set out with a business idea for making a quick buck–while pretending it was for a noble cause. When the business didn't reach its goals, instead of sticking it out, these entrepreneurs left. I have a hard time calling them entrepreneurs. For when the situation got tough, they went packing. Sure, I can understand leaving if continuing with a venture means personal bankruptcy or social disaster. But these people left because they weren't making the amazing amounts of money they expected to make in a short time. The entrepreneurial spirit wasn't there. Unless a freak accident was to occur, success was surely going to elude these people.

It takes a lot for success to occur. However, most importantly, entrepreneurs must realize that in order to be successful, entrepreneurs must embrace failure.

Success without some sort of failure is almost unheard of. Whether it is the failure of a new product to achieve mass appeal, or the failure of a website to acquire the traffic necessary to generate the revenues needed for expansion, failure will be encountered. However, the key is to how an entrepreneur responds to failure that will determine, in the end whether they are successful, or not.

When encountered with failure, it is most important to learn from the failure. Entrepreneurs need to ask themselves: Why did it occur? How can it be prevented? Is it possible for this failure to re-occur? The facts is, if entrepreneurs ignore failure or brush it off as nonsense, or, offer a poor excuse with no reasonable backup such as "The market just isn't ready for our product!" then the failure experience will be more painful than it should have been. After the 9/11 terrorist attacks, many dotcoms, who were on their last legs, blamed the 9/11 terrorist attacks for the reason their businesses failed. All too often I would log onto FuckedCompany.com (a popular website which lists all the dotcoms that went out of a business) and see excuses such as "The 9/11 terrorist attacks created less demand for our product." While it is, perhaps, a reasonable excuse for travel companies, I personally find it morally repulsive that a site offering online movies blames the terrorist attacks for lowering demand or a site offering online games with no real business model closes down because "9/11 created a hostile business climate!" While I've changed the nature of the businesses to protect them, it is very interesting to see how businesses and entrepreneurs react to failure. Mind you, these companies never talked about how on 9/10/2001 they were nearing the end of their cash reserves and had little or no customers.

In my opinion, these people aren't entrepreneurs. Instead of learning from their previous mistakes (Why did they have so few customers in the first place? How could they have changed it around? Did they get feedback from their existing clientele?) Each company found an excuse to get out nearly unscathed and exploited the tragic events of 9/11. By blaming an event that is not related to their business, entrepreneurs and businesses were able to "gracefully" exit the business and entrepreneurial world. The going got tough and they got scared. The entrepreneurs couldn't deal with rejection/failure. They didn't know how to handle it. Because of this, success eluded them, and will continue to elude them until they are able to honestly look back, see how they failed, and learn from their experience.

The fact is, I've dealt with so much failure I don't think I'd be able to fit it all into this book. I've dealt with everything from advertisers defaulting on payments, to relying too heavily on certain clients, to dealing with outright fraud, to very unscrupulous investors who continued to lie and make promises they couldn't keep. Many of these failures took a great personal toll on me. I will admit that due to some of the dealings with investors, I became depressed and began to question my abilities, my goals, and my life. It wasn't fun–I thought I was a failure and that my entire life in business was ruined.

Dwelling on these problems deepened my depression. I was only able to improve my outlook once I took some action and took a proactive stance, turning the negatives into positives. I had to learn from my experiences and prepare myself for what was to come next. I looked at the investor situation and needed to figure out why they treated me so poorly–why wasn't I able to command respect from them? By looking over logs of conversations (and I have to admit, this was a very painful process) I was able to see what I was doing wrong. By identifying the problem and acting on it, I was preparing myself to deal with future investors. By examining all my failures, and understanding what I needed to change, I emerged a stronger person (it does build character). It has helped me greatly in my current endeavors (working with a NYC consulting firm, Primary Support Solutions and, as a student and teaching assistant at Boston University).

During the height of my depression, I began to think that it might be time to switch career paths and pursue criminal justice or psychology–respectable, stable fields where a secure income was possible. Hmmmm. Then I would not have to deal with all the bs that goes along with business. I think that I possibly could be successful in another field. However, my definition of success differs with the possible success I could achieve in the more traditional fields. By creating my own definition of success, I have the strength and vigor to continue to pursue my interest and true love–business. I am, following my bliss.

For entrepreneurs, and for that matter, for anyone, it is important to create one's own definition of success. Everyone's definition of success is different. It is something to strive for and, to know, to never be fully satisfied until the goal is reached. (You know, really, reach for the stars). When things are looking down, it is important to look at your definition of success so you know what you are looking for (these are what we call defining moments). A definition of success needs to be based on a person's skill and aspirations. An expert chef should not define success as "Being in the NBA" unless the chef has the time, effort and necessary skill to play in the NBA. Instead, setting a goal such as "Being the executive chef of a four star restaurant" would probably be a more realistic definition. This will help comfort the chef when he/she is taking complex cooking classes and wondering why they are putting themselves through this. It will help to ease the chef when he/she is watching a television cooking show and taking notes and wondering why on Earth they are taking notes while watching a chef on television cook shrimp.

To fully understand the whole process of success, I asked Devin Lazerine, of Rap-Up to share some of his secrets of success. Devin, at age 15, established a goal: to create a print magazine. Through hard work and determination, Devin was able to secure a contract and ultimately have a magazine with a circulation of 200,000. Today, at age 19, Devin is the editor in chief of Rap-Up magazine and has a staff of 16 (6 fulltime employees, 10 part time employees).

Q. How do you define success in business?

Devin Lazerine: I define success in business as setting goals and meeting those goals. Set out to achieve something and actually achieve what it is you want. Success can also be defined by how well you do something. It is determined by the individual.

Q. Can you tell me about some of the failures you encountered?

Devin Lazerine: Many doors were closed on me when I first went about trying to find a publisher for Rap-Up. I heard many people say no before I got one to say yes. I wouldn't exactly call these failures, but failed attempts. When requesting interviews with some high profile artists, I was turned down by some initially. It's hard to accept failure so early on, but as time goes on, you learn to deal with it.

Q. Do you consider yourself successful?

Devin Lazerine: I consider myself successful, but still am very much a work in progress. There is still a lot more I want to achieve before I am satisfied.

Q. What steps did you to do strive to success?

Devin Lazerine: Determination and hard work helped me become successful. I knew what I wanted and I wasn't about to let anything get in the way of that. I was willing to do anything to reach my goal.

Q. How did you deal with failure?

Devin Lazerine: Don't let failure discourage you. I have learned a lot from the failures including what to do and what not to do next time. I won't let myself think of failing as the end of the world. That will only discourage you. If something doesn't work out, go on to the next thing. There's no time to waste dwelling in failures. That time can be used toward something productive. Pick up the pieces and move on.

I am going to conclude this chapter with an essay I wrote in my senior year of high school. It is an essay about success, which was written 13 days after the tragedy of 9/11. At this point, my radio business was launching, but a major problem with an investor occurred.

English Composition
9/24/2001

Success

Almost any magazine and/or media outlet contains articles and advertisements suggesting what success is–a new car, a big house, a big promotion, or a fancy new boat. Honestly, when one begins to examine one's view of success one cannot help but be influenced by all that surrounds him or her: Pat Robertson defines true success as knowing God first, family second and business third; businesses may define success by profit growth and customer satisfaction; Jim Goodman, President and CEO of Capital Broadcasting defines one who is successful as being committed, forthright and involved; and Ralph Waldo Emerson defines success in *Because You Have Lived* as: to know that even one life has breathed easier—this is to have succeeded.

All the above views of success contain values and ethics, which truly bring out the best in man. A careful examination of each variation of success shows one's own values and ethics at work.

Truly, a successful person can't be put into one category. Society may label someone who is able to garner large amounts of money as someone who is successful. It is this writer's opinion that a truly successful person is one who encompasses many traits. A truly successful person is someone who is socially healthy and stable, one who is well balanced, and prosperous both financially and spiritually. None of these traits should be mutually exclusive, but rather should merge into one true self.

Success isn't merely an accumulation of material goods. It may not even be being CEO of a prestigious worldwide company. This view, coming from one whose dream is to be a successful entrepreneur may be surprising to some. But this writer contends that success is not just "getting there" but should rather be redefined as the *process* in getting there, *how* one gets there, and *earning* the right to be there. Success cannot be considered success if one attains the top of his or her field at the expense of others, ethically, morally, or legally. Success cannot be attained at any cost.

This is not to say being the head of a company cannot be defined as a successful person, if he or she earned the right to be there and continues to earn his or her wings each day thereafter. Progression, success and growth cannot be measured alone by the title on the office door.

Each person needs to discover his or her own definition of success. In order to do so, one first needs to define his or her own values and ethics. Nothing is impossible and nothing can impede the flow of success if one remains true to himself.

The intent of this paper is not to advocate a retreat from ambition and achievement. It is only this writer's opinion that society needs to consider broadening the modern definition of success to more than just a corporate grade.

5

The Round Table

In the round table, all the entrepreneurs profiled answered a variety of questions about business. Some of the questions asked are specific questions about each entrepreneur's business, while other questions deal with general business issues. The full text of each entrepreneur's interview is located in the appendix of the book.

Devin Lazerine is the founder and editor-in chief of the nationwide hip-hop and R&B focused magazine, Rap-Up. Launched in July 2001, the full-color, glossy publication has a circulation of 200,000 and is available at newsstands and retail stores throughout the U.S. and Canada. Writers from Rolling Stone, VIBE, The Source, XXL, CosmoGIRL! and more, have all contributed to the publication.

Rap-Up is originally based upon Lazerine's concepts and website, Rap-Up.com. He started the website and magazine at age 15 while still in high school.

Bryan Hammond is the co-founder and CEO of ExploreAnywhere Software, LLC. ExploreAnywhere Software is a software firm based in New Hampshire specializing in computer monitoring, security and privacy applications in the windows environment. Some of the media mentions for the firm include Fortune Magazine, PC Magazine, CNN, BBC and Computer User.

The story of ExploreAnywhere is about a teenager who turned his love of programming from a hobby into a viable business. Today, ExploreAnywhere is enjoying a successful run on top of the PC monitoring software market and currently has one of the most downloaded pieces of PC monitoring software on the Internet.

Aaron Greenspan is the President & CEO of Think Computer Corporation, as well as the company's Founder. He started the company from his bedroom in Cleveland, Ohio in 1998. From 1998-2001, Aaron grew Think Computer's consulting operations to support more than 150 businesses, individuals and schools across the United States and Canada. In October of 2000, he spearheaded the creation of Think Computer Foundation <http://www.thinkcomputer.org>, a 501(c)3 non-profit organization with the goal of helping children through technology. Aaron is the recipient of the 1999 Junior Achievement Young IT Entrepreneur of the Year Award.

He was also awarded the Kodak Young Leaders award, and has spoken at the NASA Kennedy Space Center. Aaron currently attends Harvard University, where he is studying economics.

Q. What are the names of your companies?

Devin Lazerine: Rap-Up

Bryan Hammond: ExploreAnywhere Software, LLC

Aaron Greenspan: Think Computer Corporation

Q. What are your websites?

Devin Lazerine: http://www.rap-up.com

Bryan Hammond: http://www.exploreanywhere.com.

Aaron Greenspan: http://www.thinkcomputer.com

Q. What are some of the other companies any of you have worked for? What are your experience levels?

Devin Lazerine: Previous experience writing for a couple magazines and running other websites.

Bryan Hammond: Some of my previous jobs included being a dishwasher, bus boy, store baggage clerk (bag boy), pizza maker and a retailer at CompUSA. Basic teenaged jobs.

Aaron Greenspan: Babysitter, computer camp counselor.

Q. How old are each of you now?

Devin Lazerine: 19. I started when I was 15.

Bryan Hammond: 18. I started programming when I was 12. I started the business officially when I was 17.

Aaron Greenspan: 20. I started when I was 11.

Q. This is for Devin: You first started at the age of 15. What inspired you to start the website/magazine?

Devin Lazerine: I always wanted my own business and I thought what better way to get started than to do something that I enjoy. Music was an obvious choice for me. I was knowledgeable about hip-hop and R&B so it made perfect sense. The website was created with a bigger picture in mind—the magazine.

Q. This is for Devin: How did you learn how to make the website? How did you learn about the magazine business?

Devin Lazerine: I taught myself to make a website. When I was 13, I started using the computer more frequently for schoolwork which led to my interest in creating a website. I learned HTML by experience. Most people use programs for their sites, but I actually was able to do it without a program. That was the best way to learn because it taught me the foundation for building a site.

I am still learning about the publishing industry. Each day I learn something new. Just like the website, I learned about the magazine business through experience. With the first issue, I acted as the founder and editor-in-chief of Rap-Up. Now I am the publisher as well and with that title comes a lot more responsibility. I am having to deal with things that I didn't before such as advertising, circulation, budgets, etc. I am now involved with both the business and creative sides of publishing.

Q. How has owning a business changed each of you?

Devin Lazerine: Starting *Rap-Up* has opened me up to so many new experiences that I would have never imagined possible before. Not only has it made my life busier, but I have been able to do things that most people my age don't get the chance to do. It has also provided me with skills that I can use for the rest of my life. Owning a business can be a learning process. I am learning new things every day by experience.

Bryan Hammond: Owning my own business has taught me to think through decision much more carefully, and make the best choice possible. It has also given me the ability manage my own life, finances, etc at such a young age, where most people don't start doing that sort of thing until they are out in college.

Aaron Greenspan: Aside from spending more of my time on issues that relate to the business and being aware of business terms and practices, I don't believe Think Computer has changed me much at all. I did not start the business in order to facilitate a change in my personality. Rather, a combination of my traits led to me starting the business.

Q. This is for Devin: You say owning a business is a learning process. What kinds of things are you still learning? What do you desire to learn? What are some things you've learned that you don't feel you could of learned in school?

Devin Lazerine: I am learning to deal with disappointment, which there is always a lot of in this business. It's hard when you are first starting out to hear so many "no's." You can't let that discourage you though. If you keep at it, eventually you will get what you want.

I still would like to learn more about the record industry so I have taken up a couple internships. A&R, marketing, publicity, and promotions are all areas of interest to me.

Again, I think experience is a major learning process. I have learned so much from actually doing things than I ever did being told what to do.

Q. Have any of you been discriminated because of your age? If so, how have you overcome it?

Devin Lazerine: Yes, there have been times when I first started out and wasn't able to get interviews and meetings because of my age. Age can also be used to your advantage though. Sometimes, others don't want to deal with a teenager and other times they will be more likely to give you a shot because of your age.

Bryan Hammond: Yes. Most people do not take me serious when they see me, because I am an 18-year-old entrepreneur. But, once I begin to explain to them what I do, the software, and the press/media recognition either myself or the company has received, they take me serious and want to hear more and more.

Aaron Greenspan: Before I incorporated Think Computer, which took place when I was fifteen years old, I often encountered adults who did not believe that I could fix computers as I claimed.

Q. How did you guys overcome the age discrimination?

Devin Lazerine: If you act professional, no one should discriminate against you based on age. Over time, Rap-Up built up a good reputation and age no longer was an issue.

Aaron Greenspan: The obvious way to circumvent this problem was to prove them wrong. Dealing with adults who were insecure because of my computer-related knowledge posed another difficulty, but fortunately, I eventually graduated from all of the schools where I found that to be a problem.

Q. How do fellow classmates/friends perceive each you? Have any of your relationships changed as a result of owning the business?

Devin Lazerine: My friends think it's great that I have accomplished what I want at such an early age. A few relationships did change though. Upon realizing what I do, others thought I was the one acting different when in fact it was they who had changed their attitude towards me. They started to look at me different.

Bryan Hammond: Most of my classmates are happy for what I have accomplished and enjoy to hearing about the success I have achieved.

Aaron Greenspan: I would think that my friends perceive me as they perceive all of their other friends, but I don't actually know how others perceive me. With the notable exception of friends who have worked for me in the past, I would hope that my company has not changed my relationship with any of them.

Q. This is for Devin: Are you upset at the relationships that changed?

Devin Lazerine: I am not upset at the relationships that changed. At least now I know whom I can trust and who I can't. It shows who your true friends are.

Q. How do teachers/parents perceive each of you?

Devin Lazerine: My teachers and parents perceive me as the same person I was before I had the magazine.

Bryan Hammond: Teachers are generally enthusiastic and like to hear about everything I have done, as well as what my plans are for the future and what I plan to do with the business.

Q. How were each of you able to win over support of your parents?

Devin Lazerine: When my parents actual saw the first issue of Rap-Up in front of them, they realized that I was making my dream come true. The physical proof was enough to win them over.

Q. How exactly are each of you managing your time?

Devin Lazerine: Since I run the magazine while attending school I have to try and get my classes scheduled in the early morning so I can be back and still have time to work. It can be difficult, especially since most of the people I deal with are in NY.

Bryan Hammond: I basically put business before everything else. When I feel like I have done enough in a day, or I've achieved what I set out to do that day business wise, I will then go hangout with my friends and be social. What's your work schedule like? How many hours of week? Do you stay up late or wake up early because of your business? My work schedule isn't set in stone. But basically, if I'm not out with friends, I'm working. I work all day, go out at night, and then resume working when I get home at night until 4am or so. Sometimes I won't go to sleep at all, and work till 6 or 7am and then take a nap and resume the work process once I wakeup around noontime.

Q. What's are your individual work schedule like? How many hours of week? Do you guys stay up late or wake up early because of your business?

Devin Lazerine: I work around 40—50 hours a week, that's not including the amount of time I am in school. I try to wake up early and always end up working late till the early hours of the morning including weekends.

Aaron Greenspan: It varies depending on the time of year. During the school year I might spend as little as an hour per week on the company specifically. Homework always comes first. During the summer, I work on a completely different schedule to accommodate the various projects I'm working on. Then, I tend to fall asleep closer to 2:00 A.M., and try to wake up around 10:00 A.M. or later whenever possible.

Q. This is for Devin: You are working a full time schedule of 40 to 50 hours a week. Has that had any affect on your grades?

Devin Lazerine: Yes, it has had its toll on my grades in the past. You would be able to tell when my schedule got hectic because my grades tended to be lower around that time. I learned my mistake though and am making sure it doesn't have a continued effect.

Q. Do any of you have nightmares because of your business? Does it keep any of you up at night?

Devin Lazerine: I don't usually have nightmares about my business. Thankfully, I have only had dreams where good things happen to my company. I sometimes find it hard to fall asleep when something is on my mind. I am constantly thinking about *Rap-Up* and it keeps me up at night.

Bryan Hammond: Nope.

Aaron Greenspan: No.

Q. Who is your most prestigious client?

Devin Lazerine: We really don't have clients. It is more of dealing with publicists at record labels such as Island/Def Jam, Sony Music, J, Jive, Universal, Arista, etc.

Aaron Greenspan: Harvard University

Q. Have any of you met any celebrities because of your business?

Devin Lazerine: Yes, since *Rap-Up* is a national hip-hop and R&B magazine, I have had the chance to meet and interview many celebrities including Mariah Carey, P. Diddy, Destiny's Child, Lil' Kim, Mya, Monica, Fabolous, Nate Dogg, and many more. These are some of the perks that come along with the job.

Bryan Hammond: My software was reviewed by Leo Leporte on TechTV. That's as close as I've come to a celebrity.

Aaron Greenspan: I had the opportunity to have breakfast with Guy Kawaski, who was a member of the original Macintosh team at Apple Computer, Inc.

Q. Who is the most impressive (or top 2 or 3) CEO's each you have spoken with?

Devin Lazerine: Clive Davis (CEO, J Records), Paul Caine (Publisher, Teen People), and Robert Gregory (Publisher, Rolling Stone).

Bryan Hammond: The CEO of Digital River

Aaron Greenspan: When I was thirteen years old I e-mailed Jerry Kaplan, CEO of the now-defunct GO Corporation, who responded. When I was fifteen years old I e-mailed Bill Gates, Chairman of Microsoft Corporation, who did not respond.

Q. This is for Bryan: The CEO you met, did it help inspire you anyway for your business?

Bryan Hammond: He just gave me the basic advice—don't blow your money away, always stay on top, and makes sure the business is as best it can be.

Q. What has been your inspiration for the business? Who has helped you out the most?

Devin Lazerine: People like Clive Davis, P. Diddy, and Russell Simmons have inspired me because they have created empires and been successful at whatever they do. My family has helped me out the most by being there and supporting me. Also, H&S Media, *Rap-Up*'s first publisher, who gave me the chance to make my dream a reality.

Bryan Hammond: My inspiration is just seeing how much success I can achieve. Since my business is software, being able to code ANYTHING gives me to drive to proceed. If things weren't a challenge, I wouldn't be interested. It's all about writing the best software possible and getting it out there to be successful.

Aaron Greenspan: I don't know that there was a single inspiration for the business, and no single person has helped me the most. I've relied on my family and my friends for help when I've needed it.

Q. What made each of you think of the ideas for your business?

Bryan Hammond: I saw other companies offering software that I felt could be improved on. The software was buggy, and didn't offer all of the features I thought were necessary to make the application as best it could be. So—I set off and began writing my own software from scratch. I kept in tact of all the "standard" features in the market, and then added my own to make it better and different.

Q. How have each of your parents dealt with the business?

Devin Lazerine: When first starting out, my parents were not too happy about me pursuing something other than school. They wanted to make sure I was 100% focused on my studies. Over the last couple years they have changed their attitudes toward the magazine to a more positive one.

Bryan Hammond: They were skeptical at first, now they are very thrilled and help out in any way that they can (accounting, odd jobs, etc)

Aaron Greenspan: Though my mother was slightly worried at first, both of my parents have always been very supportive of me running the company. They have both provided significant guidance whenever I've needed it. Since my mother works at home, I've always had a frame of reference to work off of.

Q. What's the coolest kind of tech gadget each of you have had?

Devin Lazerine: iPod and Motorola Timeport P935

Bryan Hammond: iPaq PocketPC

Aaron Greenspan: My digital camera, a five-megapixel Canon PowerShot S50.

Q. How many palm pilots have each of you owned? Have they helped?

Devin Lazerine: I only owned one Palm Pilot when I first started out, but then quickly switched to a 2-way because it was easier to retrieve my emails wirelessly. The Palm Pilot did not help as much as the 2-way.

Bryan Hammond: I just purchased my first Pocket PC recently, and I'm already addicted. I'm sure I'll be purchasing more down the line as the technology for these devices increase.

Aaron Greenspan: One, though it was invented before the Palm Pilot came into existence. My middle school band director gave me his Tandy Z-PDA in eighth grade (1996) because it was too slow to keep track of his own calendar. Not surprisingly, it was also too slow to keep track of mine. It was the first PDA ever to run software developed by Palm, Inc. I now keep track of my weekly calendar during the school year with a pen and paper.

Q. What is everyone's future plans? College?

Devin Lazerine: I am currently attending college and plan to transfer to a university in the next year or so. I want to branch out into other areas of the music industry while pursuing my education. Some of my goals include running a record label, TV show, and other magazines.

Bryan Hammond: Yes, I will be attending the Whittemore School of Business at the University of New Hampshire. During this time, I will continue to further my business in every way possible.

Aaron Greenspan: This fall I will be a junior at Harvard College. After college, I hope to run Think Computer full-time.

Q. This is for Bryan: Was it hard to choose college over working full time for your business?

Bryan Hammond: Yes. I was very tempted to not go to college and pursue the business full time, going to the next level. But, I decided that it would be best to have a college education under my belt in the event that I would have to work for someone else someday down the line if I am unable to run this (or another) business.

Q. Do any of you plan to ever work for someone? Or will you try to avoid it at all costs?

Bryan Hammond: I plan to never work for anyone. I have yet to not achieve a goal, so I doubt this one will be a problem—seeing as what I have achieved thus far in my life, and only being 18 years old.

Aaron Greenspan: I certainly may work for someone in the future, but I'll do my best to continue working for myself.

Q. This is for Devin: You mentioned some of your other goals (such as a TV show, record label, etc etc). How do you feel you are going to achieve those objectives? Is it going to be hard to stray from your main product (the magazine) and into new areas?

Devin Lazerine: I am working with an agent to pitch the TV show so it alleviates a lot of work on my part. The record label will have to wait a little longer though until I can focus on getting it started. The magazine is and will always be my #1 priority.

Q. Do any of you have a projected retirement age?

Devin Lazerine: I don't have a projected retirement age. I really enjoy doing what I do and can't see myself not working for a long time to come. If you enjoy what you do, I think most people won't think of retiring so soon.

Bryan Hammond: Nope. I love working. I can't picture myself not working.

Aaron Greenspan: No.

Q. This is for Devin: You mentioned you have 6 full time employees and 10 part time. What are the ages of the part time and full time employees?

Devin Lazerine: The full time employees are in their late 20's, early 30's and the part time ones range between 17 years old and mid to late 20's.

Q. (For Devin) Are they in an office or work from home? How did you find/hire them?

Devin Lazerine: With the first issue, we had an office with the publishing company in LA and Chicago. Right now, I am working from a home office until we have the need to expand. The fulltime employees worked for the publisher before Rap-Up and the part time ones were found by recommendations or through the Internet.

Q. How are each of you able to balance your social life?

Devin Lazerine: I make time to spend with my family and friends. Spending time with them is very important to me so I always make sure I have my priorities right. In the past, I have missed out on things, especially in high school, because of the magazine's demanding schedule.

Bryan Hammond: I always find time to hangout with my friends, or spend time with my family. While my schedule can be demanding (keeping up with everything), I don't always have as much time as I would like—but I always find time for something whenever possible.

Q. Are any of you able to go out?

Devin Lazerine: Yes, I make sure I have the right balance between work and taking time off. Some of my work responsibilities include attending concerts and industry events so that is a great way to take time off while still working.

Bryan Hammond: Yes, I always find time to go out and enjoy life with my friends and family. What good would life be if you weren't able to find some time to enjoy yourself? As long as you work hard, there is no reason why shouldn't be able to play hard!

Q. Do any of you reserve time each week/month/day to do normal, social activities

Devin Lazerine: Yes, definitely. Each week I make sure I don't overdo the workload so that I have time to go out. The summer is a perfect time to catch up on social activities since I am not attending school.

Q. Do any of your friends/family/boyfriend/girlfriend feel alienated?

Devin Lazerine: In high school, some of my friends felt alienated, but since I started college, that is no longer the case. The high school schedule was more demanding because it was 5 days a week. My family does not feel alienated because I see them every day.

I barely have time to meet girls than I do to date one, but if someone like Beyoncé was to call me tomorrow, I'd make time. :)

Q. What's the best advice you guys would give to any teenager wishing to start a business?

Bryan Hammond: Put in the effort, have a good solid idea, and roll with it. Don't expect to make big bucks right away. That was possible 5 years ago, but not today. If you have a good idea, and you can stand behind it, there is no reason why you cannot achieve success.

Aaron Greenspan: Make sure you're not starting a business to make money, to impress your friends, or for no reason at all. The best businesses are those that are structured around a solid, profitable idea, and a reliable, responsible entrepreneur. Think about whether your idea and your personal characteristics can make a business run. It's not very hard to start a business. It's just a matter of finding a good lawyer, a good accountant, and the right IRS forms. Finding all of those things are the hard part.

Q. This is for Devin: can you give us some pointers for breaking into the magazine business?

Devin Lazerine: When I was 15, I started a website called Rap-Up.com. My ultimate goal was to develop the site into a print magazine after I had graduated from college. However, I didn't want to wait that long and less than a month after launching the site, I started pitching my idea to a few publishers. Sure enough, I received a call from the CEO at H&S Media. He asked to meet with me on a recent trip to LA. We met at the Beverly Hills Hotel for breakfast and he was surprised and impressed by just how young I was (16 at the time). From there, I was introduced to the H&S Media staff and began to set up interviews and hire writers. I worked with publicists to secure these interviews and built up my own contacts. Rap-Up had its premiere issue on newsstands in July 2001.

My advice on how to break into the magazine biz—persistence and hard work.

Below are some recent articles on me that might be helpful.

USA WEEKEND

http://www.usaweekend.com/03_issues/030309/030309lazerine.html
Entrepreneur:
http://www.entrepreneur.com/Your_Business/YB_SegArticle/
0,4621,299288——8-,00.html
L.A. Daily News & Sydney Morning Herald (Australia):
http://old.smh.com.au/news/0107/19/entertainment/entertain10.html

APPENDIX A

Interview with Devin Lazerine

RAP-UP

Rap-Up is the nationwide hip-hop and R&B magazine founded by 19 year-old editor-in-chief Devin Lazerine. Launched in July 2001, the full-color, glossy publication has a circulation of 200,000 and is available at newsstands and retail stores throughout the U.S. and Canada. Writers from Rolling Stone, VIBE, The Source, XXL, CosmoGIRL! and more, have all contributed to the publication.

Rap-Up is originally based upon Lazerine's concepts and website, Rap-Up.com. He started the website and magazine at age 15 while still in high school.

Here's a sample of what Devin's schedule is like:

Weekday schedule:

5:30 AM—Wake Up
6:30 AM—Work/Check emails/make calls to NY
8 AM—2 PM—School
2—7 PM—Work/Meetings/Interviews
7 PM—Family/Dinner
8—11 PM—Work/Writing Features/Planning

As you can see, Devin lives a very crazy life and he has an amazing story to tell. So without further ado, here is the interview I conducted with him. Devin's responses to the questions are **bolded**.

Q. What is your name and company?
Devin Lazerine and the company is *Rap-Up*

Q. What's your website?
www.rap-up.com

Q. What are some of the other companies you have worked for? What is your experience level?

Previous experience includes writing for a couple magazines and running other websites.

Q. How old are you now?
19

Q. You first started at the age of 15. What inspired you to start the website/magazine?

I always wanted my own business and I thought what better way to get started than to do something that I enjoy. Music was an obvious choice for me. I was knowledgeable about hip-hop and R&B so it made perfect sense. The website was created with a bigger picture in mind—the magazine.

Q.How did you learn how to make the website? How did you learn about the magazine business?

I taught myself to make a website. When I was 13, I started using the computer more frequently for schoolwork which led to my interest in creating a website. I learned HTML by experience. Most people use programs for their sites, but I actually was able to do it without a program. That was the best way to learn because it taught me the foundation for building a site.

I am still learning about the publishing industry. Each day I learn something new. Just like the website, I learned about the magazine business through experience. With the first issue, I acted as the founder and editor-in-chief of Rap-Up. Now I am the publisher as well and with that title comes a lot more responsibility. I am having to deal with things that I didn't before such as advertising, circulation, budgets, etc. I am now involved with both the business and creative sides of publishing.

How has owning a business changed you?

Starting *Rap-Up* has opened me up to so many new experiences that I would have never imagined possible before. Not only has it made my life busier, but I have been able to do things that most people my age don't get the chance to do. It has also provided me with skills that I can use for the rest of

my life. **Owning a business can be a learning process. I am learning new things every day by experience.**

You say owning a business is a learning process. What kinds of things are you still learning? What do you desire to learn? What are some things you've learned that you don't feel you could of learned in school?
I am learning to deal with disappointment which there is always a lot of in this business. It's hard when you are first starting out to hear so many "no's." You can't let that discourage you though. If you keep at it, eventually you will get what you want.

I still would like to learn more about the record industry so I have taken up a couple internships. A&R, marketing, publicity, and promotions are all areas of interest to me.

Again, I think experience is a major learning process. I have learned so much from actually doing things than I ever did being told what to do.

Have you been discriminated because of your age? How have you overcome that?
Yes, there have been times when I first started out and wasn't able to get interviews and meetings because of my age. Age can also be used to your advantage though. Sometimes, others don't want to deal with a teenager and other times they will be more likely to give you a shot because of your age.

How did you overcome the age discrimination?
If you act professional, no one should discriminate against you based on age. Over time, Rap-Up built up a good reputation and age no longer was an issue.

How do you fellow classmates/friends perceive you? Have your relationships changed?
My friends think it's great that I have accomplished what I want at such an early age. A few relationships did change though. Upon realizing what I do, others thought I was the one acting different when in fact it was they who had changed their attitude towards me. They started to look at me different.

Are you upset at the relationships that changed?
I am not upset at the relationships that changed. At least now I know who I can trust and who I can't. It shows who your true friends are.

How do teachers/parents perceive you?

My teachers and parents perceive me as the same person I was before I had the magazine.

How were you able to win over support of your parents?

When my parents actual saw the first issue of Rap-Up in front of them, they realized that I was making my dream come true. The physical proof was enough to win them over.

How exactly are you managing your time?

Since I run the magazine while attending school I have to try and get my classes scheduled in the early morning so I can be back and still have time to work. It can be difficult, especially since most of the people I deal with are in NY.

What's your work schedule like? How many hours of week? Do you stay up late or wake up early because of your business?

I work around 40—50 hours a week, that's not including the amount of time I am in school. I try to wake up early and always end up working late till the early hours of the morning including weekends.

You are working a full time schedule of 40 to 50 hours a week. Has that had any affect on your grades?

Yes, it has had its toll on my grades in the past. You would be able to tell when my schedule got hectic because my grades tended to be lower around that time. I learned my mistake though and am making sure it doesn't have a continued effect.

Do you have nightmares because of your business? Does it keep you up at night?

I don't usually have nightmares about my business. Thankfully, I have only had dreams where good things happen to my company. I sometimes find it hard to fall asleep when something is on my mind. I am constantly thinking about *Rap-Up* and it keeps me up at night.

Who is your most prestigious client?

We really don't have clients. It is more of dealing with publicists at record labels such as Island/Def Jam, Sony Music, J, Jive, Universal, Arista, etc.

Have you met any celebrities because of your business?

Yes, since *Rap-Up* is a national hip-hop and R&B magazine, I have had the chance to meet and interview many celebrities including Mariah Carey, P. Diddy, Destiny's Child, Lil' Kim, Mya, Monica, Fabolous, Nate Dogg, and many more. These are some of the perks that come along with the job.

Who is the most impressive (or top 2 or 3) CEO's you have spoken with?

Clive Davis (CEO, J Records), Paul Caine (Publisher, Teen People), and Robert Gregory (Publisher, Rolling Stone).

What has been your inspiration for the business? Who has helped you out the most?

People like Clive Davis, P. Diddy, and Russell Simmons have inspired me because they have created empires and been successful at whatever they do. My family has helped me out the most by being there and supporting me. Also, H&S Media, *Rap-Up*'s first publisher, who gave me the chance to make my dream a reality.

How have your parents dealt with the business?

When first starting out, my parents were not too happy about me pursuing something other than school. They wanted to make sure I was 100% focused on my studies. Over the last couple years they have changed their attitudes toward the magazine to a more positive one.

What's the coolest kind of tech gadget you have had?

iPod and Motorola Timeport P935

How many palm pilots have you owned? Have they helped?

I only owned one Palm Pilot when I first started out, but then quickly switched to a 2-way because it was easier to retrieve my emails wirelessly. The Palm Pilot did not help as much as the 2-way.

What are your future plans? College?

I am currently attending college and plan to transfer to a university in the next year or so. I want to branch out into other areas of the music industry while pursuing my education. Some of my goals include running a record label, TV show, and other magazines.

You mentioned some of your other goals (such as a TV show, record label, etc etc). How do you feel you are going to achieve those objectives? Is it going to be hard to stray from your main product (the magazine) and into new areas?

I am working with an agent to pitch the TV show so it alleviates a lot of work on my part. The record label will have to wait a little longer though until I can focus on getting it started. The magazine is and will always be my #1 priority.

Do you plan to ever work for someone? Or will you try to avoid it at all costs?

I would never rule out working for someone. If it means landing a job at a major record label, I would be up for it. I have done a couple internships at labels while running *Rap-Up* as well.

Do you have a projected retirement age?

I don't have a projected retirement age. I really enjoy doing what I do and can't see myself not working for a long time to come. If you enjoy what you do, I think most people won't think of retiring so soon.

You mentioned you have 6 full time employees and 10 part time. What are the ages of the part time and full time employees?

The fulltime employees are in their late 20's, early 30's and the part time ones range between 17 years old and mid to late 20's.

Are they in an office or work from home? How did you find/hire them?

With the first issue, we had an office with the publishing company in LA and Chicago. Right now, I am working from a home office until we have the need to expand. The fulltime employees worked for the publisher before Rap-Up and the part time ones were found by recommendations or through the Internet.

How are you able to balance your social life?

I make time to spend with my family and friends. Spending time with them is very important to me so I always make sure I have my priorities right. In the past, I have missed out on things, especially in high school, because of the magazine's demanding schedule.

Are you able to go out?

Yes, I make sure I have the right balance between work and taking time off. Some of my work responsibilities include attending concerts and industry events so that is a great way to take time off while still working.

Do you reserve time each week/month/day to do normal, social activities?

Yes, definitely. Each week I make sure I don't overdo the workload so that I have time to go out. The summer is a perfect time to catch up on social activities since I am not attending school.

Do your friends/family/boyfriend/girlfriend feel alienated?

In high school, some of my friends felt alienated, but since I started college, that is no longer the case. The high school schedule was more demanding because it was 5 days a week. My family does not feel alienated because I see them every day.

I barely have time to meet girls than I do to date one, but if someone like Beyoncé was to call me tomorrow, I'd make time. :)

I have also asked Devin to share his expertise and knowledge about the magazine business. Here is what he said:

When I was 15, I started a website called Rap-Up.com. My ultimate goal was to develop the site into a print magazine after I had graduated from college. However, I didn't want to wait that long and less than a month after launching the site, I started pitching my idea to a few publishers. Sure enough, I received a call from the CEO at H&S Media. He asked to meet with me on a recent trip to LA. We met at the Beverly Hills Hotel for breakfast and he was surprised and impressed by just how young I was (16 at the time). From there, I was introduced to the H&S Media staff and began to set up interviews and hire writers. I worked with publicists to secure these interviews and built up my own contacts. Rap-Up had its premiere issue on newsstands in July 2001.

My advice on how to break into the magazine biz—persistence and hard work.

Below are some recent articles on me that might be helpful.

USA WEEKEND

http://www.usaweekend.com/03_issues/030309/030309lazerine.html
Entrepreneur:
http://www.entrepreneur.com/Your_Business/YB_SegArticle/
0,4621,299288——8-,00.html
L.A. Daily News & Sydney Morning Herald (Australia):
http://old.smh.com.au/news/0107/19/entertainment/entertain10.html

APPENDIX B

ExploreAnywhere Software LLC

ExploreAnywhere Software is a software firm based in New Hampshire that was founded by Bryan Hammond. The firm specializes in computer monitoring, security and privacy applications in the windows environment. Some of the media mentions for the firm include Fortune Magazine, PC Magazine, CNN, BBC and Computer User.

The story of ExploreAnywhere is one about a teenager who turned his love of programming from a hobby into a viable business. Today, ExploreAnywhere is enjoying a successful run on top of the PC monitoring software market and currently has one of the most downloaded pieces of PC monitoring software on the Internet. Bryan has a fascinating story to tell and hopefully this interview will help anyone take his or her hobby to the next step, becoming a full and thriving business.

Please tell us your name, the company and the web address for your business.
I am Bryan Paul Hammond and my company is ExploreAnywhere Software, LLC and the website address is http://www.exploreanywhere.com

Before ExploreAnywhere, what are some of your previous jobs?
Some of my previous jobs included being a dishwasher, bus boy, store baggage clerk (bag boy), pizza maker and a retailer at CompUSA. Basic teenaged jobs.

Did these jobs help you with your business or were the motivation to start your own business?

What's your current age:
18

What age did you first start your business?

Well, I started ExploreAnywhere Software when I was 17. I originally started programming software when I was 13.

How has owning a business changed you?

The way I make decisions is much different than previously, and I take different approaches to solving problems.

Have you been discriminated because of your age? How have you overcome that?

Yes. Most people do not take me serious when they see me, because I am a 18-year-old entrepreneur. But, once I begin to explain to them what I do, the software, and the press/media recognition either myself or the company has received, they take me serious and want to hear more and more.

How do fellow classmates/friends perceive you? Have your relationships changed?

Most classmates have the mentality in their head that "Oh, he drives a nice car and has a lot of money. It must be nice to be you!" They don't realize that owning your own business takes up so much of your time, it's amazing to think how I even manage to balance school, social life, and business. Classmates always like to hit me up for money too, using the excuse "you have so much money, why don't you lend me $10!". What's funny is, I never discuss my financial situation with anyone (except close friends) so they really have no idea how much I'm worth—so why are they are they guessing?

How do teachers/parents perceive you?

Teachers are generally enthusiastic, and like to hear about it. But, since I'm a slacker, I choose not to tell teachers myself because I don't want them to think that because I don't get straight A's, I'm trying to give the impression of "I'm better than you and I don't need your education" Two teacher stories

1) Philosophy teacher asked in the middle of class how much I net per year. I didn't answer him—told him only people who know my finances are my parents, accountant and lawyer.

2) Math teacher got pissed one day and said "We all can't be like Mr. Hammond and buy a new car every month.". I told him to not discuss something that he has no idea about, and to not bring up my financial situation and what I do with my money again (he apologized for being snide later that day).

How exactly are you managing your time?

I basically put business before everything else. When I feel like I have done enough in a day, or I've achieved what I set out to do that day business wise, I will then go hangout with my friends and be social. What's your work schedule like? How many hours of week? Do you stay up late or wake up early because of your business? My work schedule isn't set in stone. But basically, if I'm not out with friends, I'm working. I work all day, go out at night, and then resume working when I get home at night until 4am or so. Sometimes I won't go to sleep at all, and work till 6 or 7am and then take a nap and resume the work process once I wakeup around noontime.

Do you have nightmares because of your business? Do they keep you up at night?

Nope.

Have you met any celebrities because of your business?

My software was reviewed by Leo Leporte on TechTV. That's as close as I've come to a celebrity.

Who is the most impressive (or top 2 or 3) CEO's you have spoken with?

The CEO of Digital River

The CEO you met, did it help inspire you anyway for your business?

He just gave me the basic advice—don't blow your money away, always stay on top, and makes sure the business is as best it can be.

What has been your inspiration for the business? Who has helped you out the most?

My inspiration is just seeing how much success I can achieve. Since my business is software, being able to code ANYTHING gives me to drive to proceed. If things weren't a challenge, I wouldn't be interested. It's all about writing the best software possible and getting it out there to be successful.

What made you think of the ideas for your business?

I saw other companies offering software that I felt could be improved on. The software was buggy, and didn't offer all of the features I thought were necessary to make the application as best it could be. So—I set off and began writing my own software from scratch. I kept in tact of all the "standard"

features in the market, and then added my own to make it better and different.

How have your parents dealt with the business?
They were skeptical at first, now they are very thrilled and help out in any way that they can (accounting, odd jobs, etc).

How many palm pilots have you owned? Have they helped?
I just purchased my first Pocket PC, and I'm already addicted. Can't live without that damn thing.

What are your future plans? College?
Yes, I will be attending the Whittmore School of Business at the University of New Hampshire.

Was it hard to choose college over working full time for your business?
Yes. I was very tempted to not go to college and pursue the business full time, going to the next level. But, I decided that it would be best to have a college education under my belt in the event that I would have to work for someone else someday down the line if I am unable to run this (or another) business.

Do you plan to ever work for someone? Or will you try to avoid it at all costs?
I plan to never work for anyone. I have yet to not achieve a goal, so I doubt this one will be a problem—seeing as what I have achieved thus far in my life, and only being 18 years old.

Do you have a projected retirement age?
Nope. I love working. I can't picture myself not working.

How have you dealt with failure?
I do what I can to get by and deal with it.

What is some advice you can give to teen entrepreneurs who fail?
Don't give up. Everyone fails. If the failure is out of your control, then don't worry about it and give it a try. But, if the failure is your own doing (i.e. your too lazy, don't want to do something, cut corners, etc), you need to re-

evaluate what you are doing and decide if starting your own business is really what you want to do. Not everyone is cutout to do it.

After the interview was conducted, I asked Bryan to offer his opinions on multiple subjects in business. Here are his responses:

In regard to marketing,

What is the most cost effective method of marketing you have used?
Advertising on websites related to your content (including download sites, audience sites (like parenting, security, etc, etc)

What's the best marketing tip you can tell?
You got to spend money to make money. Do legitimate advertising, and don't fall for "too good to be true" schemes (like 10 millions hits to your website in a day, etc). These schemes give your business a bad reputation, and give rarely any results. The best advertising is done by reaching your audience (in every aspect) and finding related websites, magazines, etc that offer advertising plans.

In regard to the Internet

How has the Internet changed your business?
It has allowed me capture the eyes of billions of people. The Internet is a great thing—without it, I doubt the business would be as successful as it is.

How are you using the Internet add value to your business?
I use the Internet to market products, find ideas, advertise, etc.

How did you develop your web presence?
The website was designed by my graphic designer, but I plugged in all of the content, etc. I like to do things on my own because I am very picky. Plus, I know where to strategically place things to help entice sales and whatnot.

How do you see the Internet affecting your business?
As the Internet grows, so does the concern of cheating spouses, employee's getting off task, children talking to pedophiles, etc. All of these things are what makes my software so popular. Controversy sells. And it just so hap-

pens that my software relates directly to what everyone uses on a daily basis (the internet, chatting, etc) so it is unlikely that the Internet will cause the business to go under.

What's a pitfall most people face with their website?
Image is everything. If your site is garbage, you wont get sales. You need to pay attention to detail. If you aren't good at designing websites, hire some-one that is. If your web-presence isn't good enough, people won't trust you, and thus, people will not buy from you.

In regard to starting a business

What advice would you give teens who want to start a business?
Put in the effort, have a good solid idea, and roll with it. Don't expect to make big bucks right away. That was possible 5 years ago, but not today. If you have a good idea, and you can stand behind it, there is no reason why you cannot achieve success.

APPENDIX C

Think Computer Corporation

Aaron Greenspan is the President & CEO of Think Computer Corporation, as well as the company's Founder. He started the company from his bedroom in Cleveland, Ohio in 1998. From 1998-2001, Aaron grew Think Computer's consulting operations to support more than 150 businesses, individuals and schools across the United States and Canada. In October of 2000, he spearheaded the creation of Think Computer Foundation <http://www.thinkcomputer.org>, a 501(c)3 non-profit organization with the goal of helping children through technology. Aaron is the recipient of the 1999 Junior Achievement Young IT Entrepreneur of the Year Award.

He was also awarded the Kodak Young Leaders award, and has spoken at the NASA Kennedy Space Center. Aaron currently attends Harvard University, where he is studying economics.

What is the name of your company?
Think Computer Corporation, Think Computer Foundation

What are the URLS of your companies?
http://www.thinkcomputer.com, http://www.thinkcomputer.org

Can you tell us some of your previous jobs?
Babysitter, computer camp counselor

How old are you now?
20

What is the age when you first started?
11

Can you give us any approximate numbers in revenue?
Approximately one quarter-million dollars since the company's inception on April 29, 1998.

How has owning a business changed you?
Aside from spending more of my time on issues that relate to the business and being aware of business terms and practices, I don't believe Think Computer has changed me much at all. I did not start the business in order to facilitate a change in my personality. Rather, a combination of my traits led to me starting the business.

Have you been discriminated against because of your age? How have you overcome that?
Before I incorporated Think Computer, which took place when I was fifteen years old, I often encountered adults who did not believe that I could fix computers as I claimed. The obvious way to circumvent this problem was to prove them wrong. Dealing with adults who were insecure because of my computer-related knowledge posed another difficulty, but fortunately, I eventually graduated from all of the schools where I found that to be a problem.

How do fellow classmates/friends perceive you? Have your relationships changed?
I would think that my friends perceive me as they perceive all of their other friends, but I don't actually know how others perceive me. With the notable exception of friends who have worked for me in the past, I would hope that my company has not changed my relationship with any of them.

What's your work schedule like? How many hours of week? Do you stay up late or wake up early because of your business?
It varies depending on the time of year. During the school year I might spend as little as an hour per week on the company specifically. Homework always comes first. During the summer, I work on a completely different schedule to accommodate the various projects I'm working on. Then, I tend to fall asleep closer to 2:00 A.M., and try to wake up around 10:00 A.M. or later whenever possible.

Do you have nightmares because of your business? Do they keep you up at night?
No.

Who is your most prestigious client?
Harvard University

Have you met any celebrities because of your business?
I had the opportunity to have breakfast with Guy Kawasaki in 1999, who was a member of the original Macintosh team at Apple Computer, Inc.

Who are the most impressive CEO's you have spoken with?
When I was thirteen years old I e-mailed Jerry Kaplan, CEO of the now-defunct GO Corporation, who responded. When I was fifteen years old I e-mailed Bill Gates, Chairman of Microsoft Corporation, who did not respond.

What has been your inspiration for the business? Who has helped you out the most?
I don't know that there was a single inspiration for the business, and no single person has helped me the most. I've relied on my family and my friends for help when I've needed it.

How have your parents dealt with the business?
Though my mother was slightly worried at first, both of my parents have always been very supportive of me running the company. They have both provided significant guidance whenever I've needed it. Since my mother works at home, I've always had a frame of reference to work off of.

What's the coolest kind of tech gadget have you had?
My digital camera, a five-megapixel Canon PowerShot S50.

How many palm pilots have you owned? Have they helped?
One, though it was invented before the Palm Pilot came into existence. My middle school band director gave me his Tandy Z-PDA in eighth grade (1996) because it was too slow to keep track of his own calendar. Not surprisingly, it was also too slow to keep track of mine. It was the first PDA ever to run software developed by Palm, Inc. I now keep track of my weekly calendar during the school year with a pen and paper.

What are your future plans? College?
This fall I will be a junior at Harvard University. After college, I hope to run Think Computer full-time.

Do you plan to ever work for someone? Or will you try to avoid it at all costs?
I certainly may work for someone in the future, but I'll do my best to continue working for myself.

Do you have a projected retirement age?
No.

At the end of the interview, I asked Aaron to comment on different issues in business. Here are his responses

MARKETING

What is the most cost effective method of marketing you have used?
Word-of-mouth and the press are the two most cost-effective methods of marketing in existence.

Can you list all the forms of marketing you have used and tell of their effectiveness?
Word-of-mouth—Very high
Trade shows and conferences—Poor
Networking groups—Poor
Press articles—Very high
Print advertising—Poor
Web advertising—Very Poor
E-mail—Average

What's the best marketing tip you can tell?
Don't pay for anything if you don't have to.

FAILURE

Have you encountered failure?
Of course.

How have you dealt with failure?
I would guess the way most people do: by diagnosing the problem, fixing it or learning from it, and trying again.

What is some advice you can give to teen entrepreneurs who fail?
Everyone fails. Most people have never heard of "Traf-O-Data," despite the fact that it was owned and operated by Bill Gates—before he started Microsoft.

NEGOTIATIONS/INVESTORS

How have you dealt with investors?
I have chosen not to deal with investors. All of Think Computer's capital has come from my own work.

How did you raise the money for your venture?
I started with $3,397.00 that I raised from summer jobs and babysitting at $4.00 per hour. My parents provided $150.00 of the total sum, as well as my computer.

How do you succeed in negotiating? Do you feel you are at a disadvantage when you negotiate?
It depends on the negotiation. When I am negotiating software deals, I usually feel that I know more than the other party involved, and so I'm not typically worried. In other situations, you simply have to be aggressive to prevent the other party from discovering any weaknesses that you may have.

What's the best way to approach a negotiation? Are you generally nervous or relaxed? How do you relax yourself?
I don't get nervous until about a minute before a given event. By that time, it's too late to turn back, and so I relax by just going through with it.

THE INTERNET

How has the Internet changed your business?

Think Computer probably would never have happened without the Internet. Much of the information I found about starting a business was only available to me through the World Wide Web. Many of my customers have found me through the Internet, and some would not even be customers if the Internet did not exist since they purchase internet-related goods and services. At the present time, all of the software products that we sell to customers are web-based.

How are you using the Internet to add value to your business?

Customers can purchase Think Computer products and services over our secure web site using a credit card at http://www.thinkcomputer.com.

How did you develop your web presence? In house or outsourced?

I taught myself HTML in seventh grade, and Think Computer has had about eight versions of its corporate web site since then. We host our own web site, as well as many others.

What's a pitfall most people face with their website?

Most small businesses cannot afford an in-house Information Technology staff, and therefore have to rely on a site designer to make updates for them. Designers know this, and often charge outrageous rates to update sites as a result. We've developed Whiteboard, a program geared toward small businesses, to allow people to update their own web sites without any outside help. With a retail price of $99.00, it's much more affordable than practically any other solution on the market.

HUMAN RESOURCES

How many fulltime [sic] and part time employees do you have?

I am the only full-time employee of Think Computer. There are four other employees on the payroll.

Is it hard to manage adults when they are at your firm?

No, because there aren't any. When I work with adults who are my clients, I am not in a position to manage them, since I am performing work for them.

How do you command respect with your employees? Especially if you can't attend a meeting because of class?

I think the best way to earn the respect of your employees is specifically *not* to command it. I am extremely honest with people, and I believe that my openness is what leads people to trust me. Regarding meetings, I generally schedule them around classes so as to avoid any problem.

STARTING A BUSINESS

How hard was it to start?

It's not very hard to start a business. It's just a matter of finding a good lawyer, a good accountant, and the right IRS forms. Finding all of those things are the hard part.

What advice would you give teens who want to start a business?

Make sure you're not starting a business to make money, to impress your friends, or for no reason at all. The best businesses are those that are structured around a solid, profitable idea, and a reliable, responsible entrepreneur. Think about whether your idea and your personal characteristics can make a business run.

Thank You

Thank you to my mom, Patricia Cathers for her assistance in the editing of the book.

Thank you to my dad, Michael Cathers for financing this book.

Thank you to Howard Kroplick, CEO of the Impact Group, for his suggestions and advice on this book.

Author Biography

Ben Cathers is currently a student and teaching assistant at Boston University, School of Management. Previously, he was Co-Founder and CEO of the Teen American Media Group and CEO of phatstart.com, both companies Ben started in his teenaged years. Ben currently resides on Long Island, New York with his family.

Ben has been featured in the Silicon Alley Reporter; Yahoo Internet Life; Revu Magazine; Gas Pedal Ventures Magazine; The Sunday London Times; Fox News; The Long Island Herald; The Debra Dunkins Show and The Megs and Modems Radio Show. Ben is also the youngest person ever to be the CEO of a company that received Silicon Alley Reporter's distinction of being named as one of the top 12 companies to look out for.

Ben can be reached at http://www.bencathers.com

0-595-29410-3